Bookkeeper School

Pre-QuickBooks®

How to Save Tax Dollars

By Gina D'Amore

Published by
Hybrid Global Publishing
301 E 57th Street, 4th fl
New York, NY 10022

Copyright © 2017 by Gina D'Amore

All rights reserved. No part of this book may be reproduced or transmitted in any form or by in any means, electronic or mechanical, including photocopying, recording, or by any information storage and retrieval system, without the written permission of the Publisher, except where permitted by law.

Manufactured in the United States of America, or in the United Kingdom when distributed elsewhere.

D'Amore, Gina
    Bookkeeper School: Pre-QB, How to Save Tax Dollars
    ISBN:
    Paperback: 978-0-692-89619-8
    eBook: 978-1-938015-79-3

Back Cover photo by: YELENA: Photographer of JOY
Permission credits: Reprinted with permission © Intuit® Inc. All rights reserved.

www.lovesaccounting.com

Introduction

Accounting...Bookkeeping...

Confused? Don't know where to begin? Creative accounting...Enron and Bernie Madoff did that... serious consequences.

I've seen QuickBooks® entries so creative there is just simply no logic to it.

Would you like to put some logic in your creative accounting?

Awesome!

This book is a pre-QuickBooks lesson.

This is where to begin.

QuickBooks is as easy to use as Microsoft Word (once you learn the pictures ☺) Okay, it's slightly more complicated than that, but not much.

QuickBooks is easy you, just need to know a few basics first. My favorite part is it is logical ☺ It really can be easy. No, really! Logical and easy. Some basic vocabulary like P&L, which means profit and loss statement, and you will even sound like you know what you are doing ☺

About the Author

I am a Michelangelo of numbers. This is my passion. Think of me as an angel that fell from the stock market into her calling.

No one ever said life was going to be easy, and wow it's not easy! I graduated at the top of my class in economics and worked in the stock market until that moment when over half a million stock market workers lost their jobs in 2 months immediately after the 2008 crash.

Accountants are the last to go ... instantly back to school I went!

I was trained to analyze what accountants produced so that was a logical choice. 4.0gpa on all 3 degrees within 1 ½ years: bookkeeping certificate, a certified tax preparer (I did a tax season – No, thank you), and an associate degree in accounting. Yeah, from bachelors I went backwards, no one has ever accused me of being normal!

It was the middle of an economic crisis, I had no experience in accounting, but I could analyze it. I dummied down my resume to get an unpaid internship ... within 6 months I was a manager.

With my driving ambition and now 5 top honors college degrees on my resume, I climbed the company ladder to financial controller within a few years. Oh, I got a human resources certificate along the way, figured I should know what I am doing. I mean Cali is the strictest of all 50 states and federal law, and they seem to change wage laws every 6 months lately.

Coming from a woman that didn't set her life goals out to learn accounting either, but it is necessary, we will get through this together.

My Daddy always said,

"How do you eat an elephant?

One bite at a time.".

Table of Contents

What is an expense? 10
Office Expenses versus Office Supplies 13
List of How to Save Money 15
- ♥   H.S.A. or F.S.A. 16
- ♥   Meals and Entertainment / Travel 19
- ♥   Inventory 25
- ♥   Bonuses 27
- ♥   Education 29
- ♥   Payroll into College 529 or Retirement 31
- ♥   Auto Deduction 34
- ♥   Charitable Contributions 37
- ♥   Retirement Contributions 38
- ♥   Distributions 41

♛ STORY ♛ 43

Rent your House up to 15 days 46
Sole Proprietor and Medical as of 2016 (since 2017) 48

♛ Story Alert ♛ 49

Part 2

CHART OF ACCOUNTS	51
Subaccount	55
Business Expenses need to be both ordinary and necessary	61
Items and Services	72
Story	78
Accounts Payable	79
Accounts Receivable	81
Call QuickBooks	82
♥ Rules of Thumb ♥	83

Bookkeeper School

Pre-QuickBooks

How to Save Tax Dollars

By Gina D'Amore

What is an expense?

Before you can start entering things into any accounting system, such as QuickBooks, you will need to know what you can and cannot enter.

Ordinary and Necessary

The IRS has decided that a business expense needs to be ordinary or necessary.

That is a very broad definition of a business expense.

- ♥ Is it ordinary to your type of business?

- ♥ Is it necessary for you to do business?

First off, everyone gets the definition of ordinary and necessary, correct?

Massage therapists would be able to expense the laundry for the sheets they lay their clients on. This is ordinary and necessary expense for a massage therapist.

Mobile Notary workers would be able to expense the business use of the car.

They would use a mileage log, actual expenses with a percentage of personal use, or actual expenses 100% business use; depending.

When an accountant says it depends, it truly depends on several factors. There needs to be an entire picture surrounding the situation for there to be a solid answer from an accountant.

The above mobile notary "it depends" would depend on:

1) How you recorded the 1st year the car is used for business,

   a) Standard Mileage means using a log to record your mileage,

   or Actual Expenses using receipts.

   β) If you used Standard Mileage (recording it in a log), then you have the option of switching back and forth for whichever gives you the higher deduction.

   χ) If you took Actual Expenses, then you have to continue using receipts the entire time this car is in the service of that business.

Lawyers would expense the bar association dues and the continuing education they are required by law to take.

Each business will have different ordinary and necessary expenses.

What is necessary and ordinary...

Pens and paper are obvious necessities to an office, but what about those people that are mobile and do not have an office and truly only use technical devises?

♥ Was it for business?

If you can answer yes to this question, then it counts as a business expense.

With these really broad definitions of ordinary and necessary, I feel the need to discuss several specific items.

Office Expenses versus Office Supplies

<u>Office Supplies</u> are literally the things necessary to doing business.

- ♥ Pens
- ♥ Paper
- ♥ bottles of water
- ♥ coffee
- ♥ tea
- ♥ snacks, such as fruit, power bars, or junk food (Staples sells junk food)

<u>Office Expenses</u> are what I like to refer as the things that make doing business easier. I like to use this as my "Miscellaneous", for things when I don't know where else to put them.

- ♥ Office decorations
- ♥ Delivery services such as the water
- ♥ Membership fees such as Sam's Club or Costco
- ♥ Shredding services

- ♥ The things you don't know where else to put
- ♥ Flowers for the office
- ♥ Services for watering the plants or feeding the fish at the office

List of How to Save Money

Let's talk about what is not obvious and is still deemed ordinary and necessary.

- ♥ H.S.A.
- ♥ Travel
- ♥ Bonuses
- ♥ Inventory
- ♥ Education
- ♥ Distributions
- ♥ Auto Deduction
- ♥ Charitable contributions
- ♥ Retirement contributions
- ♥ Meals and Entertainment
- ♥ Rent your house up to 15 days
- ♥ Payroll into college 529 or Retirement
- ♥ Medical for you and kids up to the age of 27

(Isn't this list so pretty in this order, we will be discussing it out of order.)

♥ H.S.A. or F.S.A.

A Health Savings Account (H.S.A.) and a Flexible Spending Account (F.S.A.) are tax free dollars spent on health.

These might become less attractive as the new law passed stating as of 2016, Sole Proprietors can expense their medical for themselves and their children up to the age of 27. Which is a reason many Sole Proprietors had previously paid the $800 to become an S Corporation. S Corporations can just hire their family and expense their medical through the company.

But not everyone is a Sole Proprietor, and literally anyone can take advantage of an H.S.A. If offered through their place of employment, an F.S.A.

A Health Savings Account (H.S.A.) is tax free money put into a bank account specifically used for medical expenses. This money does not need to be used in a specific time frame, and can be used on any member of the family. The limit to how much you can put into this account in 2017 is $3,400 for an individual, or for the family it's $6,750. If you are 55 or older there is an additional $1,000 allowed.

Flexible Spending Account (F.S.A.) is done through an employer program, and has a limit of $2,600 in 2017. FSA dollars are generally taken from the paycheck before taxes are taken out. The money needs to be used in the year taken from paycheck (unless the $500 roll over to the next year rule applies to your specific policy). The FSA can also be used for eligible dependents. As this is done through an employer program, there will be specifications.

Sole Proprietors as of 2016 can now deduct up to 100% of health insurance premiums for themselves and dependents under the age of 27. This also includes chiropractors, psychologists, acupuncture, insulin, false teeth, eyeglasses or contact lenses, hearing aids, the transportation to receive medical care, and long-term care insurance...just to rattle off a few. The list goes on, and there are some "it depends" in there of course.

The biggest "it depends" on the Sole Prop medical expenses is the floor. There used to be a minimum of 10% of your income needed to be medical expenses before you could deduct any medical expenses (7.5% for 55+). Now the rule is the medical expenses are not covered if your company has a loss.

To put it clearer, your medical expenses cannot bring you below $0. If you have a net profit, then you may deduct 100% of health insurance premiums and other qualified medical expenses.

♥ Meals and Entertainment / Travel

First let me tell you the most important thing to know about meals and entertainment. It is only a 50% deduction up to 10% of your income.

If you have a loss, none of that counts!

The second most important thing to remember is there are 3 ways to write off meals and entertainment, depending on the circumstances.

Was it necessary?
Was the meal while you were out of town?

Were you out of the office for more than 4 hours? This gets a meal break by California human resources law.

Did you need to stop to rest after 2 hours? This gets at least a snack break by California human resources law.

A meeting or travel expense is more appropriate than an entertainment expense for meals that are necessary.

Businesses have meetings, conventions, trade shows, and business trips. The expenses on a business trip add up quickly. There is the main mode of transportation to get there, possibly an airplane or train. Don't forget the baggage fees. Then there is the taxi. Now you arrive at the hotel. This is when I suggest you use that pen and paper waiting for you at the hotel to write down all the tips you just gave.

Yes, tips are an ordinary part of a business trip, and they are 100% an expense. Just write it down. Write the date, the amount, and what it was.

Example:

2/18/2017   Taxi tip $4

Business trip meals are 100% deductible. This includes beverages, taxes and tips. Dry cleaning and laundry are a travel expense. Tipping the maid at the hotel counts, don't forget to write it down.

The next page is an IRS publication to back up what I just said.

May I please point to the last words on the IRS document, "operating and maintaining a house trailer".

Ordinary and necessary… if it can fulfil those criteria, it counts as an expense.

Table 1-1. Travel Expenses You Can Deduct

This chart summarizes expenses you can deduct when you travel away from home for business purposes.

IF you have expenses for...	THEN you can deduct the cost of...
transportation	travel by airplane, train, bus, or car between your home and your business destination. If you were provided with a free ticket or you are riding free as a result of a frequent traveler or similar program, your cost is zero. If you travel by ship, see *Luxury Water Travel* and *Cruise Ships* (under *Conventions*) for additional rules and limits.
taxi, commuter bus, and airport limousine	fares for these and other types of transportation that take you between: • The airport or station and your hotel, and • The hotel and the work location of your customers or clients, your business meeting place, or your temporary work location.
baggage and shipping	sending baggage and sample or display material between your regular and temporary work locations.
car	operating and maintaining your car when traveling away from home on business. You can deduct actual expenses or the standard mileage rate, as well as business-related tolls and parking. If you rent a car while away from home on business, you can deduct only the business-use portion of the expenses.
lodging and meals	your lodging and meals if your business trip is overnight or long enough that you need to stop for sleep or rest to properly perform your duties. Meals include amounts spent for food, beverages, taxes, and related tips. See *Meals* for additional rules and limits.
cleaning	dry cleaning and laundry.
telephone	business calls while on your business trip. This includes business communication by fax machine or other communication devices.
tips	tips you pay for any expenses in this chart.
other	other similar ordinary and necessary expenses related to your business travel. These expenses might include transportation to or from a business meal, public stenographer's fees, computer rental fees, and operating and maintaining a house trailer.

https://www.irs.gov/publications/p463/ch01.html#en_US_2015_publink1000266 0

The *IRS publications have been modified in bold and italics and <u>underlined</u>* to point out some obvious, but often overlooked expenses.

On the next page, let's start talking about Entertainment...

Table 2-1. When Are Entertainment Expenses Deductible?

General rule	You can deduct ordinary and necessary expenses to entertain a client, customer, or employee if the expenses meet the directly-related test or the associated test.
Definitions	Entertainment includes any activity generally considered to provide entertainment, amusement, or recreation, and includes meals provided to a customer or client *An ordinary expense is one that is common and accepted in your trade or business.* *A necessary expense is one that is helpful and appropriate.*
Tests to be met	Directly-related test • Entertainment took place in a clear business setting, or • Main purpose of entertainment was the active conduct of business, and • You did engage in business with the person during the entertainment period, and • You had more than a general expectation of getting income or some other specific business benefit. Associated test • Entertainment is associated with your trade or business, and • Entertainment is directly before or after a substantial business discussion • You cannot deduct the cost of your meal as an entertainment expense if you are claiming the meal as a travel expense. • You cannot deduct expenses that are lavish or extravagant under the circumstances.
Other rules	*You generally can deduct only 50% of your unreimbursed entertainment expenses (see 50% Limit).*

https://www.irs.gov/publications/p463/ch02.html

The IRS expects you to wine and dine and entertain your clients, customers, and employees. Yes, you should show appreciation to your employees by spending company money on them. Showing employees appreciation is said to lead to greater productivity.

What is lavish and extravagant under the circumstances? It depends. Use common sense, and if you ran out of that, ask an accountant. I would ask you how much money you expect to make from this and how much did you spend, the answer in a percentage would tell me if it was worth the return on the investment. If it was not, I would call that lavish and extravagant.   If you spent 10% of what you thought you would make in the next few years, that is reasonable. If you spent 40% of what you expect to make from it, that is lavish and extravagant.

- ♥ Inventory

Are you reading between the lines here?

Cash basis businesses only…

QuickBooks records the date the check was written.

Ok, I will spell it out for you. 12/31 is a great day to print checks if you have money in your bank account and you are a cash basis business.

What is cash basis versus accrual basis?

Cash basis means you record it in your accounting when it actually happens.

Accrual basis means you pay taxes on money you didn't get yet but invoiced out for already. And if you don't get that money in the future, you will have to "bad debt expense" it to get that tax money back.

Inventory is an asset on your balance sheet that every year companies pay business property tax on. Here in sunny paradise San Diego, the property tax is 1%.

Therefore, when I am tax planning with my clients, I assess their position in December. This allows me to buy inventory or other necessary things with money in the year I am trying to lower my tax liability. By spending the money, you don't have to pay taxes on it.

Of course, only buy something you need, such as inventory.

Yes, to save a lot of money, you have to have a lot of money to save.

But year-end is when companies dump hundreds of thousands of dollars, and the reason is tax avoidance. Instead they are buying ordinary and necessary things, giving bonuses, or paying taxes on the income. Let's continue this discussion in the next topic, bonuses.

♥ Bonuses

Do you like your employees or Uncle Sam Better?

In my mind it is not a holiday bonus, it is an end of the year decision.

If there is money in the bank account in December (or year-end), then the accountant knows it needs to be spent or taxed.

While many large corporations budget for bonuses, I personally deal with the real world where people are scraping by. I actually pull up on Yahoo Finance large corporations balance sheets for my clients to show them the millions or billions of debt large companies have. The debt of large corporations is impressive, and calming to the average person.

Bottom line is everyone is trying to make their bottom line between 5%-10%. There are company cars, company bonuses and other necessary and ordinary expenses to spend the money on.

Instead of giving chunks to Uncle Sam, buy equipment or what the company needs.

Reward the company and its employees for making the bank account positive.

Employees are said to be assets, treat them well, logically they should treat you well back...so the theories in human resource management go.

- ♥ Education

Continuing Education, this is a legitimate expense. And one of the only few remaining you can pick and choose whom to give it to. Most employee benefits need to be given to all employees, or it cannot be considered necessary or ordinary any longer. The benefits must be for all staff, or just upper management is now a rule. And then there needs to be a clear line of upper and lower management, written down...oh so many details.

The automobile expenses and education can be given to the select few you prefer, such as yourself, hired family members, or whomever you select.

Education expenses before you got into your business doesn't count. Student loans just do not count unless you started the company and then went for CONTINUING education.

An accountant and lawyer both need a specific amount of hours of training per year to keep their licenses. This would be education required by law, and is very much a business expense.

Education to improve an existing career is also a business expense.

Sending an employee to college to train for a different and higher position is a legitimate business expense.

Of course, if you are not providing this for family members, there are contracts you can make employees sign to remain in your service for a specific time frame (such as 10 years) or to pay back the education expenses. College is a very pricy item, and the ROI (return on investment) needs to be protected as much as possible.

Education to qualify someone in a new trade or business does NOT qualify as a business expense.

Example, paying for your 18-year-old to go to college, totally doesn't count. But if you hire them, put them on payroll, you can actually send the entire paycheck into a college 529 plan. Next, this awesome IRS rule.

♥ Payroll into College 529 or Retirement

A college 529 plan is a tax-free investment vehicle for college savings to grow, specific per state, with slight differences. This is often started by a grandparent and is how and where anyone can contribute to a child's college fund. The 529 plan can pay for college in any location. The money goes into the 529 plan tax free, grows, and comes out tax free as long as it pays for college expenses (which now include books and Starbucks). $14,000 is the limit per year, unless it is the person that is going to use it contributing. Self-contributions have no limit.

Let us back into this idea for a moment. You can put your kids on payroll. They can do something in the office. A 6 month old can hold your business card and you can post that on Facebook. Now you have incurred a modeling fee. Up to $6,300 is tax free income (each year changes). I suggest you have the money before writing a 6 month old a check, oh and it actually needs to go into their bank account. You cashing your baby's check is called embezzlement. Hey, you have control of the money anyways, go get a separate bank account for the kids so you don't get in trouble for stealing your own money.

The next level of tax bracket is 10% for about $12,000 (changes yearly). Would you rather have your kid pay for school lunches from their own bank account with money that was taxed at 10%? Or are you in love with giving Uncle Sam that higher percentage? It is not a child labor issue to over pay your own kids to take out the office trash and change the copier paper in the office.

Let's flip the script and say you are supporting your parent. Pay them into their retirement fund. If you have parents like mine, I am sure your parent will not hesitate to consult you on how to make your business better in some way ~.*

Payroll into retirement is tax free. The money is then taken out at the applicable tax bracket of the person. There are many details and retirement types. This is when I say, talk to an accountant for details.

Paying family members is not illegal. But at least have them come in and change the copy paper so it is not a complete lie.

The owners of the companies are dictated to have fair and reasonable salaries, not employees. The

IRS doesn't actually say anywhere what a fair and reasonable salary is though, use common sense.

♥ Auto Deduction

Business owners can pick and choose whom they give auto allowances to. Fairness of all employees or all upper management rules do not apply here. This is me trying to avoid blatantly saying, give the company car to the kids and wife.

Standard Mileage

versus

Actual Expenses

Standard Mileage = you record a mileage log for all business related trips

Actual Expenses = you have receipts for all auto expenses

If you used Standard Mileage the 1st year, then you have the option of switching back and forth for whichever gives you the higher deduction.

If you took Actual Expenses the 1st year, then you have to continue using receipts the entire time this car is in the service of that particular business.

71% is 5 days out of 7, which is the percentage of business use versus personal (29%), assuming you work 5 days a week and own 1 car.

You will have to only take 71% of the receipts for auto expenses and make a journal entry in QuickBooks to match your tax return.

The journal entry would look like:

Auto Expenses   credit - the math calculation of 29% of auto expense,

                lowering total expenses, raising your income.

Distribution debit - the math calculation of 29% of auto expenses,

                raising your tax liability.

Auto Expenses and Distribution will be in your "Chart of Accounts" which is in the next section of this book.

Owners Equity/Distributions/Owners Draw – it depends on what type of company you are. QuickBooks will fill that blank in for you, don't worry.

It is much easier to do actual expenses since a mileage log is tedious, but actual does not always give you the best deduction.

You can depreciate a company car, within limits, if you buy it as a company vehicle in the company's name.

♥ Charitable Contributions

Companies and people can make charitable contributions, and this would lower your tax liability. Unless you have a loss or you have to choose to carry forward.

Carry Forward

Carry forward is when you need to take a period of time to complete the taxable event.

If you have a loss in your company, you can spread that loss over several years.

Oh, it depends doesn't even begin to start how much everything depends on this one. If you have a loss, call someone.

♥ Retirement Contributions

I can't even count how many retirement investment types there are, and I count for a living. They each have specific rules and maximums.

Let me explain. If you have a company with employees and you start a 401(k) plan, there is compliance. This compliance needs to be done by a third party administrator (TPA) by law. These TPA's are costly. The compliance is detailed.

To summarize, if you fail a compliance test, it will cost you thousands of dollars on top of the thousands of dollars it costs to run the compliance test...that you must run annually.

If you are a small company, your chances of failing a compliance test are great.

Compliance, a certain dollar amount in each employment level must be satisfied.

Example:

Upper management puts in the max of $16k

Lower employees put in a total of $500

Now the upper management will get half their money back, and get taxed on it, because lower employees didn't put in enough.

The company has failed the compliance test, and needs to pay to take it again. That will be at least $4,000.

(Don't forget the angry employee at the top level that planned on saving for retirement, but got half back, and then had to pay the taxes.)

Simple IRA and Simple 401(k) can be held for free, and doesn't need to comply or be tested.

Here is a link to avoid that Third Party Administration (TPA) that will be costing several thousand a year.

https://individual.troweprice.com/public/Retail/Retirement/Small-Business-Retirement-Plans/SIMPLE-IRA

KEEP IT SIMPLE!!!!!!

There are several companies that will hold a Simple IRA or Simple 401(k) plan for you.

SEP IRA (Simplified Employee Pension) – up to 25% of each employee's pay – I recommend this one before you get employees.

As I said, there are too many retirement vehicles to discuss, you will qualify for a particular few. There are people paid to advise you about this no matter where you call, they should answer your questions.

- ♥ Distributions

S Corp Distributions are taxed at your ordinary income tax rate.

- ♥ Distributions avoid the 15.3% self-employment tax

IRS RULE * you must pay yourself a fair and reasonable salary*

Let me quote the IRS, twice, from the same page:

https://www.irs.gov/uac/wage-compensation-for-s-corporation-officers

"a salary amount must be determined and the level of salary must be reasonable and appropriate."

"There are no specific guidelines for reasonable compensation in the Code or the Regulations."

Any questions? Ha ha! I love the IRS website!

To put it simply, most people have no understanding of a distribution.

Sole Proprietorships do not get distributions, ever. There is no such thing in the Sole Prop world.

S Corps are typically trapped in a spiral of having to take more distributions to pay taxes on the money they took. Please don't treat your company like a bank account and then look shocked when the taxes are due.

💗 STORY 💗

My clients literally ask me "where did the money go?".

This is when I could be a 6-year-old wearing a girl scout uniform and still seem sarcastic….

I pull up what is called a "Statement of Cash Flow" and it is there; extremely clear in black and white; where the money went.

Every date, every amount

- in a list, like a clear report of what exactly happened.

And oh, that list gets very long over the course of a year.

Only $20 here and $40 there…yeah, that adds up to be A LOT!

Owners that use their company like an ATM machine are not the sharpest knives in the drawer. It is not my fault they spent all the money. I didn't put $20 in their pocket every time they got gas, and then the credit card statement BOLDLY states they took cash. If the accounting books do not reflect that $20 as an owner's distribution, then it is called illegal embezzlement.

If you take cash, you get the privilege of paying taxes on that.

This is when I pray I don't have to get the calendar out to mandatorily pay a payment plan to the IRS.

The calendar is to show and budget for the now monthly payments. Monthly payments owners are now forced to make. Forced because the IRS shows the company has now defaulted on the taxes.

Why, because they do not have the money to pay the taxes. They took it and spent it already. This is a very difficult place to be.

(And kind of embarrassing in front of your accountant. Especially when all you did was go to bars and get stupid things. Hey, I'm not judging you, just telling you now you must pay for that. And, um, those stupid things you like to buy...STOP IT!)

Then putting owners onto payroll is a must at this point. If not, the spiral of taking more distributions to pay taxes may never end.

Payroll is to force owners into paying taxes on the money they do get, so the spiral can stop.

At this point, if an owner doesn't start paying taxes each time, the tax liability amount only goes up and becomes more intimidating, more stressful, and the spiral will not stop. Only having to look forward to more stress.

And at some point, yes, you are human, things happen in life where it is necessary to go into debt. Just don't make that debt because you needed an overpriced drink at the bar on the company credit card.

The only distribution I let slip through my accounting is the "Maid" receipt from the ATM machine that occurs in timed increments that it is believable that the maid actually came. I care not if you are the maid.

Moral to the story: taxes are unavoidable

"S corporations should not attempt to avoid paying employment taxes by having their officers treat their compensation as cash distributions, payments of personal expenses, and/or loans rather than as wages."

https://www.irs.gov/uac/wage-compensation-for-s-corporation-officers

♥ Rent your House up to 15 days

"There is a special rule if you use a dwelling unit as a personal residence and rent it for fewer than 15 days. In this case, do not report any of the rental income and do not deduct any expenses as rental expenses."

https://www.irs.gov/taxtopics/tc415.html

IRS rules can be awesome!

If you rent your house for 14 days or less, then you get 100% of the income tax free! You will be unable to take the expenses, such as carpet cleaning, new keys made, anything the renters broke…

Many companies need to use their kitchen table as a conference room on a monthly basis for shareholder meetings or meetings to look at the accounting reports. This can be rented at the conference room rate of the near decent hotels average cost.

S corps can write a check from their company to themselves for this conference room space. It would apply to the less than 15 days rule since there are only 12 months in a year.

Bluntly:

call the local decent hotels in your area

get an average of their conference room rate

rent yourself your own kitchen space for 14 days or less

keep the money 100% tax free

If you have a conference area at your office, this will be a complete lie unless you actually do it, and then I am not sure it is now necessary since you would have somewhere else to do this at. Ask your accountant, it depends.

- ♥ Sole Proprietor and Medical as of 2016 (since 2017)

Medical for the first time ever is now a company expense for you and your dependents up to the age of 27 (age 26 and under).

The Schedule C used to dictate that anyone needed to spend more than 10% of their income on medical before it became a deduction. (7.5% for 55+)

Now the rule is that medical cannot make the tax return go below $0.

The list of what is included besides insurance premiums is long.

I will name a few: psychiatrist, psychologist, acupuncture, chiropractor, long-term care insurance.

This new law is probably linked to the fact that having health insurance is a law. Health insurance premiums are one of the largest costs a self-employed person has. This is huge. I have been unable to contain my excitement...

💓 Story Alert 💓

I am a bookkeeper with 5 top honors college degrees constantly arguing the fact that until 2016 a person could sit for the CPA exam in the state of California without any higher schooling.

I have told several people the new medical Sole Prop law, and their CPA's immediately belittling me and my job title saying it is untrue.

Well, here is to all you CPA's that imagine you are smarter than me.

I read the IRS website for fun and I am the one laughing at you when your insults backfire by clients asking me for tax preparer referrals. But go ahead, keep judging a book by its cover and title ~.*

Part 2

CHART OF ACCOUNTS

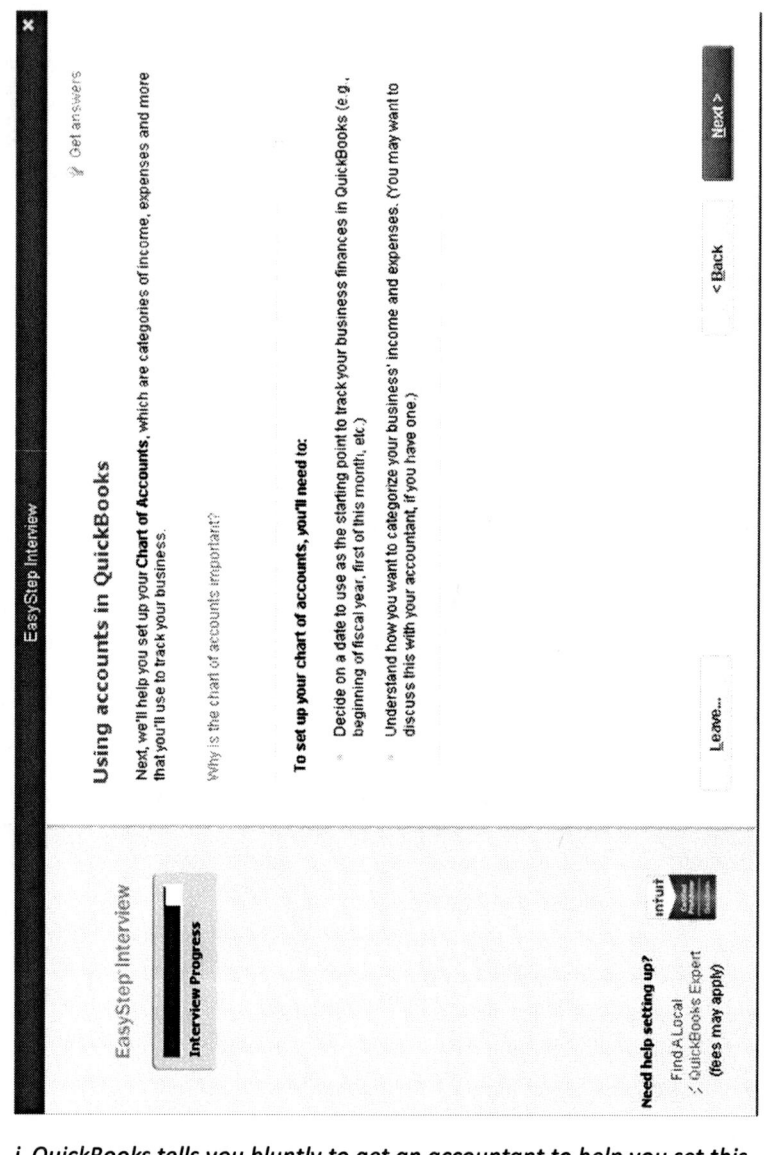

i QuickBooks tells you bluntly to get an accountant to help you set this up.

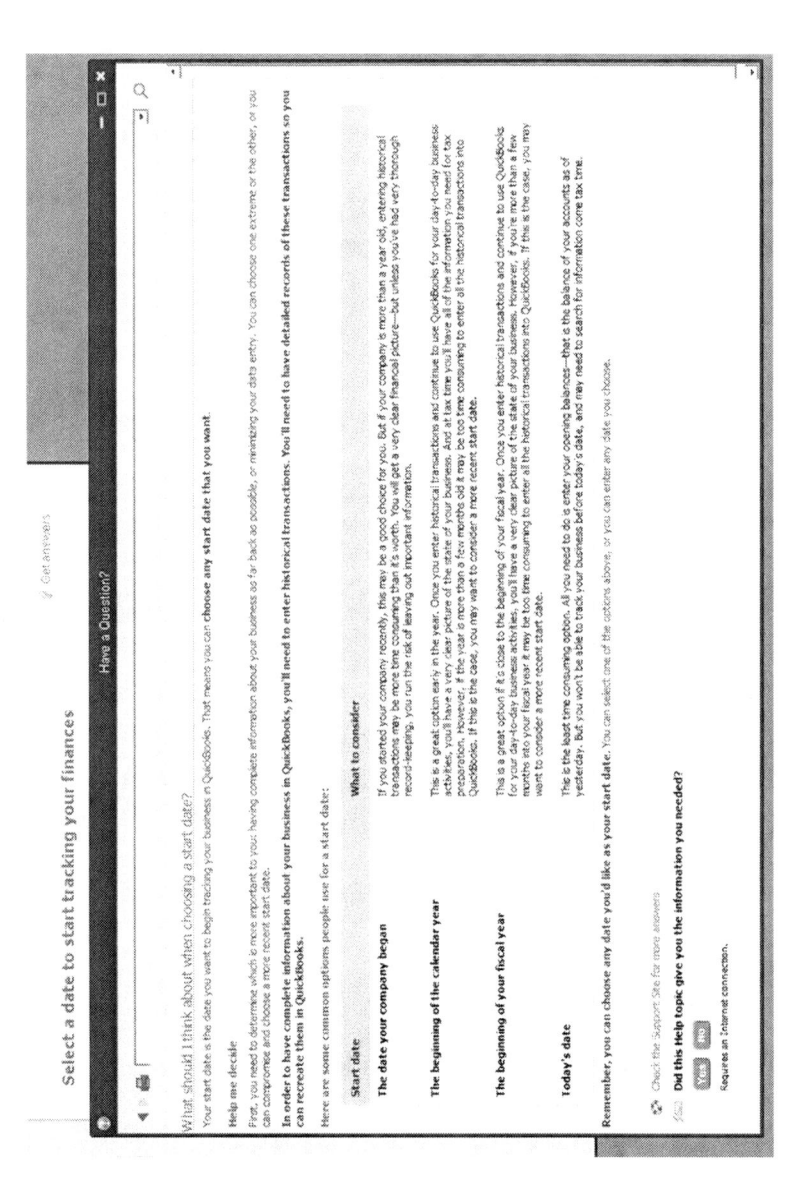

ii QuickBooks is asking for a start date...what date did you start having meetings discussing the startup plan?

Do you like your chart of accounts?

Okay, lets imagine buckets of apples and buckets of oranges.

What do you want to separate?

QuickBooks gives you a chart of accounts, yes. But it is editable.

You can make it make sense to you.

I cannot express how valuable the beginning is to the ending.

The chart of accounts are the words down the left of your financial statements. Clients repeatedly tell me they do not understand their financials. My response is they don't understand the list of buckets now full and have numbers next to them.

The Profit and Loss Statement (P&L) starts with:

Income $100,000

Okay that is simple. Let's keep it that simple.

Say you have more than one kind of income and you would like to distinguish one income from another. Ready for a vocabulary word?

Subaccount

A subaccount or subcategory is another layer of detail to differentiate whatever it is necessary to separate for analysis purposes.

Here is an example of a business that sells in different locations.

This would be helpful to analyze how much time and money should be spent on marketing.

Informed decisions come from having the information.

Income:
    Sales in store $400
    Sales online $800

    Sales at Trade shows $1,100
TOTAL INCOME: $2,300

Total income is what shows up on what you give to the banks, CPA, and the IRS. The details are just for you. So I say let's go crazy, name it what makes sense to you! I just try to encourage you to let the main category make sense to boring people. Make main categories broad, and subaccounts your details.

Automobile Expense is a common chart of account to subaccount. I tend to distinguish Automobile Expense from Auto Loan to make it easier in the end. The loan is a liability, not an expense. Baby steps, we can get to liability later.

Automobile Expense:

Gas	$100
Parking	$100
Insurance	$100
Repairs and Maintenance	$100
Tolls	$100
TOTAL AUTOMOBILE EXPENSE:	$500

It would be great to take the time to think about what you want to keep track of under a main chart of account, such as Automobile or Travel, depending on your specific company.

Miscellaneous is an account I would avoid at all costs. Business expenses need to be necessary and ordinary.

QuickBooks gives you a recommended chart of accounts.

We will learn to distinguish between the 3 main categories: Income, then Cost of Goods Sold, then Expenses.

Income is the money you receive (from customers, clients, patients, students) whatever it is you offer that Uncle Sam will want his taxes paid on. If you give your company money, I recommend putting it in a new chart of account called: LOAN from (your name here).

Cost of Goods Sold, think of it as the money you pay to sell whatever it is you sell. A home office therapist wouldn't have a cost of goods sold because they don't have a good to sell, they have a service. But if you sell toys, you have to buy the toys. The cost of the toy is a cost of goods sold. Most people that have products have inventory. Inventory becomes a cost of goods sold when you sell it, otherwise it is an asset. Assets are on the Balance Sheet, not the Profit and Loss.

<u>Expenses</u>, the necessary and ordinary costs of doing business. The warehouse or office would be a "Rent Expense". Rent expense is a chart of account that comes in your QuickBooks.

All of the chart of accounts can have subaccounts, even the subaccounts can have subaccounts.

Get your geek on with your:

6 inch tube:

x 5 inches around	1.25
with a nozzle	.75
x 6 inches around	2.00
with a nozzle	1.00

If you need a report that can spit out at the touch of a button something specific, then get specific. I just don't recommend you get too long because the above will read out like this:

6 inch tube:x 5 inches around:with a nozzle

or

6 inch tube:x 6 inches around:with a nozzle

If you enter in your cost of goods sold, QB will calculate it for you. This is entered in where you enter the product to put on the invoice. You will need to map it all correctly…start at the top, tab is your friend, answer all the questions.

Count your inventory at least in December. The tax return actually asks your beginning of the year and end of the year inventory.

Now please feel free to think of what you want to separate in your buckets/ chart of accounts. Feel free to look at your QuickBooks for their suggestions, the button is a picture on the home page on the top right. You will keep many of them, they are logical. I mean how many ways can you say Rent? Besides subaccounts for locations.

Business Expenses need to be both ordinary and necessary.

Expenses, both ordinary and necessary. Hmm…well that is very specifically broad. My chart of accounts says Meals and Entertainment…oooh…

Okay two parts, Meals and Entertainment is a 50% off deduction, up to 10% of the bottom line income you pay taxes on.

The government expects you to wine and dine your clients. But how do you know how much that 10% is going to be? You don't. Do not go out and spend an extra 10% of your income to get 5% off.

Every receipt counts if it is for anything business. Just save receipts and we will get all the tax deductions you qualify for.

Ordinary and necessary. Let's start with what a sole prop can fill in a box for (illustration of Schedule C Part II). Then, what doesn't fit in the box, your tax return would spell out your chart of account (not subaccounts) on your tax return.

Form 1040 Schedule C, Part I, Income. One number for total income, then 1 number for total returns and theft. This is where I remind

you that any return or loss accounts you create inside QuickBooks are going to need to point to an Income account not an Expense account.

Cost of goods sold is inside the income section, and is one number. This is deceiving because if you turn the page over there is a calculation to get there. This calculation uses a beginning of the year and end of the year inventory count.

Other income is interest earned, debts previously written off, and tax refunds. Don't worry, you won't have to fill this out. I am just trying to show you what the IRS sees as ordinary and necessary for every business.

SCHEDULE C
(Form 1040)

Department of the Treasury
Internal Revenue Service (99)

Profit or Loss From Business
(Sole Proprietorship)

▶ Information about Schedule C and its separate instructions is at *www.irs.gov/schedulec*.
▶ Attach to Form 1040, 1040NR, or 1041; partnerships generally must file Form 1065.

OMB No. 1545-0074

2016

Attachment
Sequence No. 09

Part II Expenses. Enter expenses for business use of your home only on line 30.

8	Advertising	8		18	Office expense (see instructions)	
9	Car and truck expenses (see instructions)	9		19	Pension and profit-sharing plans	
10	Commissions and fees	10		20	Rent or lease (see instructions):	
11	Contract labor (see instructions)	11		a	Vehicles, machinery, and equipment	
12	Depletion	12		b	Other business property	
13	Depreciation and section 179 expense deduction (not included in Part III) (see instructions)	13		21	Repairs and maintenance	
				22	Supplies (not included in Part III)	
				23	Taxes and licenses	
				24	Travel, meals, and entertainment:	
14	Employee benefit programs (other than on line 19)	14		a	Travel	
				b	Deductible meals and entertainment (see instructions)	
15	Insurance (other than health)	15		25	Utilities	
16	Interest:			26	Wages (less employment credits)	
a	Mortgage (paid to banks, etc.)	16a		27a	Other expenses (from line 48)	
b	Other	16b		b	Reserved for future use	
17	Legal and professional services	17				

Part II, Expenses

Advertising is at the top. Advertising is not only alphabetically at the top, but can be one of the largest expenses a company has. Wages is another of the highest expenses of a company.

While I mention wages and expensive, you should see the penalty for not paying the payroll tax… double. If you withhold taxes from someone's pay and do not give them to the government, the fee is the amount of the tax owed. So, if you owe $10, you now owe $20. But I digress.

Commissions and fees is an expense – oh please let me digress. I have been offered $1,000 for the first year and $500 each additional year for each client I refer to a particular payroll company. Kickback isn't the vocabulary word they use. It is referral fee, and it is very alive and well. Please trust who is selling you what.

Contract Labor expense – These are the employees you do not pay payroll tax or workers comp for, but cannot boss around much either. You cannot tell them to sit at your reception desk from 9-5. They are there to perform a specific task that is spelled out and billed to you for. They do it when they want to. You can put a deadline on when the work is to be completed. These people should get a 1099 if they earn more than $600 working for you.

Depreciation and section 179 is a little technical, but easy. Depreciation is to slowly expense something over time. Dictated by an accounting rule, is how long it depreciates for. 179 depreciation means you expense it in entirety in the year it was bought instead of expense it over time. Most small companies are cash basis sole proprietorships and do not have assets to depreciate. Sole props can be a hybrid that holds assets and depreciate them. $500 is the rule of thumb starting point to depreciate something.

Employee Benefit Programs – this is where you want to put the Employee Development sub chart of account, to expense the meal when you have an employee event at 100% and to keep track of what you spend on the most valuable assets of your company. 401(k), gym memberships, things you give every employee. There is legal compliance that comes with employee benefits. You need to have a payroll and employees before you have employee benefits.

Insurance – wow this can get expensive, but self-explanatory.

Legal and Professional services – your lawyer and accountant would go here.

Line 18 is Office expenses and Line 22 is Office Supply on the tax form. May I please quote the IRS instructions for Line 18, "Include on this line your expenses for office supplies and postage". Does the IRS make laws to confuse people on purpose?

Like I said, you aren't filling out this form. Just an example of ordinary and necessary for every business according to the IRS.

Office Expense - something not an office supply. The plant you bought to decorate, the meeting muffins, the miscellaneous expenses is what I put in here.

Office supplies - this is where I put the pens, paper, coffee, tea, snack bars, paper towels, toilet paper, water,…etc. When is the last time you walked into an office that didn't have these things?

Rent or lease – yes, most company owners lease a vehicle through the company. A company car is not always 100% a business expense. If you do not have a personal car, you will need to deduct a percentage for personal use of the vehicle. But if your company can afford a company car, it is one of the last things an owner can take advantage of. Besides continuing education, which is not on this list, but a legitimate company expense.

Travel - Ooh, look a subaccount on the IRS expenses for travel. and your meals can be 100% expensed. Taxi tips in cash while traveling can be written on a piece of paper with a date, amount, and description.

On the next 2 pages please find 2 of the prettiest charts I could find made by the IRS:

Chapter 1 Travel page 5: on travel expenses you can deduct.

Table 1-1. **Travel Expenses You Can Deduct**

This chart summarizes expenses you can deduct when you travel away from home for business purposes.

IF you have expenses for...	THEN you can deduct the cost of...
transportation	travel by airplane, train, bus, or car between your home and your business destination. If you were provided with a free ticket or you are riding free as a result of a frequent traveler or similar program, your cost is zero. If you travel by ship, see *Luxury Water Travel* and *Cruise Ships* (under *Conventions*) for additional rules and limits.
taxi, commuter bus, and airport limousine	fares for these and other types of transportation that take you between: • The airport or station and your hotel, and • The hotel and the work location of your customers or clients, your business meeting place, or your temporary work location.
baggage and shipping	sending baggage and sample or display material between your regular and temporary work locations.
car	operating and maintaining your car when traveling away from home on business. You can deduct actual expenses or the standard mileage rate, as well as business-related tolls and parking. If you rent a car while away from home on business, you can deduct only the business-use portion of the expenses.
lodging and meals	your lodging and meals if your business trip is overnight or long enough that you need to stop for sleep or rest to properly perform your duties. Meals include amounts spent for food, beverages, taxes, and related tips. See *Meals* for additional rules and limits.
cleaning	dry cleaning and laundry.
telephone	business calls while on your business trip. This includes business communication by fax machine or other communication devices.
tips	tips you pay for any expenses in this chart.
other	other similar ordinary and necessary expenses related to your business travel. These expenses might include transportation to or from a business meal, public stenographer's fees, computer rental fees, and operating and maintaining a house trailer.

This is where I like to point out the word "tips", then move to the next picture answering the question, "How do I prove that?".

IRS Chapter 5 Recording page 27

Table 5-1. How To Prove Certain Business Expenses

IF you have expenses for...	THEN you must keep records that show details of the following elements...			
	Amount	Time	Place or Description	Business Purpose / Business Relationship
Travel	Cost of each separate expense for travel, lodging, and meals. Incidental expenses may be totaled in reasonable categories such as taxis, fees and tips, etc.	Dates you left and returned for each trip and number of days spent on business.	Destination or area of your travel (name of city, town, or other designation).	Purpose: Business purpose for the expense or the business benefit gained or expected to be gained. Relationship: N/A
Entertainment	Cost of each separate expense. Incidental expenses such as taxis, telephones, etc., may be totaled on a daily basis.	Date of entertainment. (Also see *Business Purpose*.)	Name and address or location of place of entertainment. Type of entertainment if not otherwise apparent. (Also see *Business Purpose*.)	Purpose: Business purpose for the expense or the business benefit gained or expected to be gained. For entertainment, the nature of the business discussion or activity. If the entertainment was directly before or after a business discussion: the date, place, nature, and duration of the business discussion, and the identities of the persons who took part in both the business discussion and the entertainment activity. Relationship: Occupations or other information (such as names, titles, or other designations) about the recipients that shows their business relationship to you. For entertainment, you must also prove that you or your employee was present if the entertainment was a business meal.
Gifts	Cost of the gift.	Date of the gift.	Description of the gift.	
Transportation	Cost of each separate expense. For car expenses, the cost of the car and any improvements, the date you started using it for business, the mileage for each business use, and the total miles for the year.	Date of the expense. For car expenses, the date of the use of the car.	Your business destination.	Purpose: Business purpose for the expense. Relationship: N/A

Get a piece of paper and write it down, and there is a receipt.

Other Expenses – IRS instructions quote "include all ordinary and necessary business expenses not deducted elsewhere on Schedule C". This is why I just made you look at the boring IRS form.

You now have to name for the IRS your buckets that didn't fit on this section of the form.

Telephone is a utility according to the IRS, but I do not subaccount telephone under utility in my chart of accounts. I let the tax program or person figure out where everything goes.

From here you can make logical decisions of what you want your chart of accounts to say, and what subaccounts should be.

Just remember, if you used it for business, it is a business expense.

Please make logical decisions on your buckets/chart of accounts.

What do you want to keep track of? And how detailed?

Your chart of accounts is where everything points to. It is easy to set up. Just put a tiny bit of thought into it, and you can easily do it. QuickBooks is user friendly. Just read the prompts and think logically through it.

Add your bank and credit card accounts, they even talk to QuickBooks. To set up the talking/links between your QuickBooks and your bank or credit card, follow the prompts, or call QuickBooks to help you.

Items and Services

Now that we have your chart of accounts in, we can add your "Items and Services", just under the button for "Chart of Account" on the home page. Also, located at the top tool bar under "Lists" then "Item List".

What do you want to call your items and services?

You can subaccount, sub subaccount, subsub subaccount. Stay logical but if you need to get geeky with your items, QuickBooks gets as geeky as you need to get ☺

Example:

Items

 -Geeky computer part 1

      -With geeky fabulous upgrade

           -With lifetime warranty

           -With membership to other geeks

 -Geeky computer part 2

-With geeky fabulous upgrade

-With other fabulous upgrade

-Another fabulous upgrade

-With lifetime warranty

-Membership with other geeks

-Free membership for being awesome geek

So as you can see, this would be really long in a drop down eventually…

Geeky computer part 2:With geeky fabulous upgrade:Another fabulous upgrade

This is really not going to fit on your computer screen eventually.

Logical is a beautiful thing about QuickBooks. It's logical, you should stay with the flow.

To put in what is sold or service performed click the "Items and Services" on the top Right of the home screen in the Company section. Find the box labeled "Item" with a drop-down arrow at the bottom left to get a "New Item", or right click and click "New".

I recommend starting at the top left and tabbing through the boxes answering the questions with logical answers to add your products or professional services. Eventually you get to the lower right where there is a drop down for "Account". These are your buckets.

Depending, yes, accountants say that a lot. Depending on where it goes is what bucket you should put it in. Let me try to broadly explain. Services, something people get paid to do because they know how to do it. These should go to what kind of income you decided to put on your chart of accounts.

Maybe you are a plumber and it is logical to have buckets for the north, south, east and west income. This way you can see where the advertising dollars are paying off. The chart of accounts would have 4 subaccounts to separate the areas. Then the Items would differentiate what you did there.

Income

    North $100

    South $100

    East $100

    West   <u>$100</u>

TOTAL INCOME $400

Your Items would need to match to the different income subaccounts if you did this.

Item

    Electrical

        North

        South

        East

        West

On the drop down arrow, once selected it will appear separated with ":" between words.

Electrical:North

This is how you get things into the buckets you made ☺ See, easy. Just had to do the first step first. Now would be a great time to sit down and think of what you sell and how you want to keep track of it. What you decide is easily a click away on a report. A report you know how to read, because it is a list of your

chart of accounts that you now understand, and what is in them. Expert already. ☺

When you are done with this, you can click on sales reports. Sales reports you can read and use information from because you clearly see your top selling area or products, and worst. QuickBooks has a lot of reports that are very useful. Who can't read a top 10 sales report?

The report Sales by Item Summary even gives you the breakdown of your service or item by how many, how much, compares it to the others by a percentage, and gives you an average price.

Service / Item	Quantity	$ Amount	% of Sales	Average Price
Item 1	207	$7,418.00	90.60%	$35.82
Item 2	26.9	$672.50	8.20%	$25.00
Item 3	2	$100.00	1.20%	$50.00
Total	235.8	$8,187.50	100%	$34.71

… in the click of a button, a report that gives you helpful information. Informed decisions come from having the information.

Valuable information in the click of a button. You can specify by time frames, specific items, all kinds of customizations in the reports. Once there is some data in there to show up on a report, you will play with it like a new toy and see the magic.

Story

The IRS happened! This client came to me with bookkeeping done by a receptionist, (do not let the receptionist touch your QuickBooks without training or locking permissions, please). I had to clean the accounting mess the receptionist made.

The fact that the client owed $100,000 in payroll tax because of not paying the payroll taxes for $50k was the reason an audit occurred. Yes, the fine for not paying your payroll taxes, is the amount you owe in payroll taxes: double.

Accomplished, proud, proven, I had just walked across the finish line of an IRS audit with flying colors for this client. Three of us waiting for the meeting with a new consultant to begin; I had been training a new girl to do the bookkeeping, the client and myself. The consultant sits down, rudely turns to the client and says, "I thought you said your accountant was a man, is this your bookkeeper?" I chose not to respond to this. What year will women be equal?

Accounts Payable

Prioritize your bills in order of consequence and due date. Taxes should be at the top of your priority list.

Payroll and distributions. Somewhere there is a rumor out there that distributions are taxed at a lower rate than payroll. Yes, this is true. If you're over a certain tax bracket, and pay yourself a reasonable salary. Yes, put a max on your payroll and start distributions. Become informed before you do this, and don't forget to pay the taxes on any money you take.

I cannot tell you how many clients are taking large amounts of money out of their companies and then are shocked when the tax bill comes. Then need to take even more money out of the company to pay the tax bill.

I have put several people on $0 pay payroll for months at a time because it all needs to go toward paying taxes. It becomes a game of catch up that is just easier not to play.

Catch up with bills is something most can relate to. QuickBooks has a report of when your bills are due, if you put the correct due dates in. There is also a report of when you are owed money, if you fill in that box in on the invoice when you create it.

Most companies I have worked for are doing a juggling act just like people. Running a report of when to expect money to pay the bills you owe can be calming, or give anyone an instant headache.

Lines of credit are easier to establish before it is too late. You know, when your credit is still good. The credit cards, car payment, as well as others being late or missed seem to show up on a credit report instantly. Some bills seem to be easier not to pay on time and have less consequences.

Negotiate into a payment plan, get a line of credit, prioritize by consequence, and most importantly communicate. Bills do not just go away.

Accounts Receivable

On the flip side of things, friendly reminders for receiving money are recommended. Try to email the invoice again with a friendly reminder, this must've slipped through the cracks, can I get and ETA on payment.

Picking up the phone and saying, "I realize you are the middle man, but I need some kind of information please" can get you further.

Understanding and keep the friendly tone are essential. Accounts receivable is a profession for a reason, there is a trick to it.

Call QuickBooks

QuickBooks has customer service.

You get 3 years of customer service with desktop, but their 3 years ends at the end of October when their product is launched each year.

Online has their own customer service.

I do recommend getting the desktop version from the previous year because you still get the remaining time of customer service, and I love saving money!

♥ Rules of Thumb ♥

♥ **If you cannot afford it, don't buy it!!!!** ♥

I understand you really want it, and you think you will make more money soon…buy it when you can afford it.

If it is not necessary to do business, do you really want to pay interest on that? Credit card interest can be up to 22%.

Line of credit interest is calculated daily.

♥ **Get a company credit card and or bank account** ♥

And only use the company cards for company expenses.

If you do not draw a line for the IRS between personal and business…they will look at it all.

It is much easier when you are trying to get your accounting and taxes in order to be only looking at business expenses.

Annual reports with your transactions separated into categories can be very helpful when you are looking backwards. Some credit card companies give you a very comprehensive annual report.

♥ Reconcile bank and credit cards monthly ♥

When you reconcile the accounts, it is a double check that everything is correct.

Do not reconcile until it actually reconciles. QuickBooks will do a journal entry putting the "leftovers" into "Reconciliation Discrepancy". This means there is a mistake.

♥ Creative Accounting ♥

Enron, Bernie Madoff, and maybe, just maybe, your receptionist are doing what is called "Creative Accounting".

Accounting mistakes, I don't mean to be dramatic here, but can land you in jail. The really big ones, that you do on purpose. But the fines are not fun either.

Many receptionists don't know accounting!

- ♥ Miscellaneous is a red flag ♥

Office Expense is a good catch all if you cannot think of anywhere else to put that random "necessary and ordinary" business expense.

- ♥ Get a Line of Credit before your credit doesn't let you ♥

When you really need it, it won't be there unless you plan for it.

- ♥ Your car lease can go into the company's name ♥

- ♥ Yes, the toys too

All the company toys can be in the company name. Take pictures of the employees using the toys at company events. Things like a jet ski, boat, …

- ♥ Pay payroll taxes on time ♥

The fine for not paying the payroll taxes timely, is double. If you owe $50 in payroll taxes, you now owe $100. Pay that on time, the fine is truly not worth it!

- ♥ Distributions are taxable ♥

Every $1 you use your company like a bank account for is going to be taxed. Do not look so shocked when that tax is due. I recommend paying the tax as you take the money (through payroll), or setting up an account to put the tax portion of at least 25% it into and actually paying quarterly taxes appropriate.

♥   MANY Receptionists do NOT know how to accounting 💖

I get it, they are cheaper, and QuickBooks is so simple. Yeah, well, it is so simple to mess up too. In the end you will pay someone more expensive to fix what they messed up.

And to be honest, it is sometimes easier to start the entire year over again than to try to figure out what someone who had no idea what they were doing, did. There is no logic in some mistakes, they just touched the wrong button and now have an adorable look on their underpaid faces. And now the cost of fixing it is very high. Not worth it to begin with.

With all of this advice:

Talk to your accountant, because, it depends.

Epilogue

I hope this was helpful.

I hope this helped you to understand the accounting and financial statements. Most of all I hope I helped you save money on your taxes. ☺

QuickBooks is as easy to use as any Microsoft product. Just set it up correctly and it is a wonderful tool.

Thank you! ♥

CPSIA information can be obtained
at www.ICGtesting.com
Printed in the USA
FFOW05n1306180917